I Care for My Pet

My Pet

Katie Peters

GRL Consultants,
Diane Craig and Monica Marx,
Certified Literacy Specialists

Pull
Ahead
READERS
People Smarts

Lerner Publications ◆ Minneapolis

Note from a GRL Consultant
This Pull Ahead leveled book has been carefully designed for beginning readers. A team of guided reading literacy experts has reviewed and leveled the book to ensure readers pull ahead and experience success.

Lerner Publications
An imprint of Lerner Publishing Group, Inc.
241 First Avenue North
Minneapolis, MN 55401 USA

For reading levels and more information, look up this title at www.lernerbooks.com.

Main body text set in Memphis Pro 24/39
Typeface provided by Linotype.

Photo Acknowledgments
The images in this book are used with the permission of: © ANURAK PONGPATIMET/ Shutterstock Images, pp. 8–9, 16 (left); © EugeneEdge/Shutterstock Images, pp. 14–15; © Karpova/Shutterstock Images, pp. 6–7, 16 (right); © LightField Studios/Shutterstock Images, pp. 4–5, 16 (center); © NotarYES/Shutterstock Images, pp. 12–13; © Sakura Image Inc/Shutterstock Images, pp. 10–11; © Vitaly Titov/Shutterstock Images, p. 3.

Front cover: © alexei_tm/Shutterstock Images.

Library of Congress Cataloging-in-Publication Data

Names: Peters, Katie, author.
Title: I care for my pet / Katie Peters.
Description: Minneapolis : Lerner Publications, [2023] | Series: I care (pull ahead readers people smarts - nonfiction) | Audience: Ages 4–7 | Audience: Grades K–1 | Summary: "A dog needs to be walked, brushed, and fed. Early readers can explore ways to care for a pet in this easily accessible text. Pairs with the fiction book, My Pet"— Provided by publisher.
Identifiers: LCCN 2021044323 (print) | LCCN 2021044324 (ebook) | ISBN 9781728457604 (library binding) | ISBN 9781728461526 (ebook)
Subjects: LCSH: Pets—Juvenile literature.
Classification: LCC SF416.2 .P474 2023 (print) | LCC SF416.2 (ebook) | DDC 636.088/7—dc23

LC record available at https://lccn.loc.gov/2021044323
LC ebook record available at https://lccn.loc.gov/2021044324

Manufactured in the United States of America
1 – CG – 7/15/22

Table of Contents

I Care for My Pet 4

Did You See It? 16

Index 16

I Care for My Pet

I pet my dog.

I walk my dog.

I feed my dog.

I wash my dog.

I brush my dog.

I love my dog.

How can you show you care about a pet or other animal?

Did You See It?

bowl   dog   leash

Index

brush, 13   walk, 7

feed, 9   wash, 11

love, 15